LOS GATOS PUBLIC LIBRARY
P.O. Box 949
Los Gatos, CA 95031
408 354-6891

Comets and Asteroids

Amanda Davis

The Rosen Publishing Group's
PowerKids Press™
New York

Published in 1997 by The Rosen Publishing Group, Inc.
29 East 21st Street, New York, NY 10010

First Edition

Book Design: Erin McKenna

Photo Credits: Cover © Michael Simpson/FPG International Corp.; p. 4 © Paul & Lindamarie Ambrose/FPG International Corp.; p. 7 © FPG International Corp.; p. 8 © NASA/FPG International Corp.; p. 11 © Paul Ambrose/FPG International Corp.; pp. 12, 16 © Telegraph Colour Library/FPG International Corp.; pp. 15, 19 Jack Zehrt/FPG International Corp.; p. 20 © Research Photos/FPG International Corp.

Davis, Amanda
    Comets and asteroids / by Amanda Davis
       p.   cm. — (Exploring Space)
    Includes index.
    Summary: Briefly discusses the composition and position of comets, asteroids and meteors.
    ISBN 0-8239-5059-X
    1. Comets—Juvenile literature. 2. Asteroids—Juvenile literture. [1. Comets. 2. Asteroids. 3. Meteors.] I. Title.
II. Series: Davis, Amanda. Exploring space.
QB721.5.D39 1997
523.6—dc21

                                        96–53485
                                          CIP
                                          AC

Manufactured in the United States of America

Contents

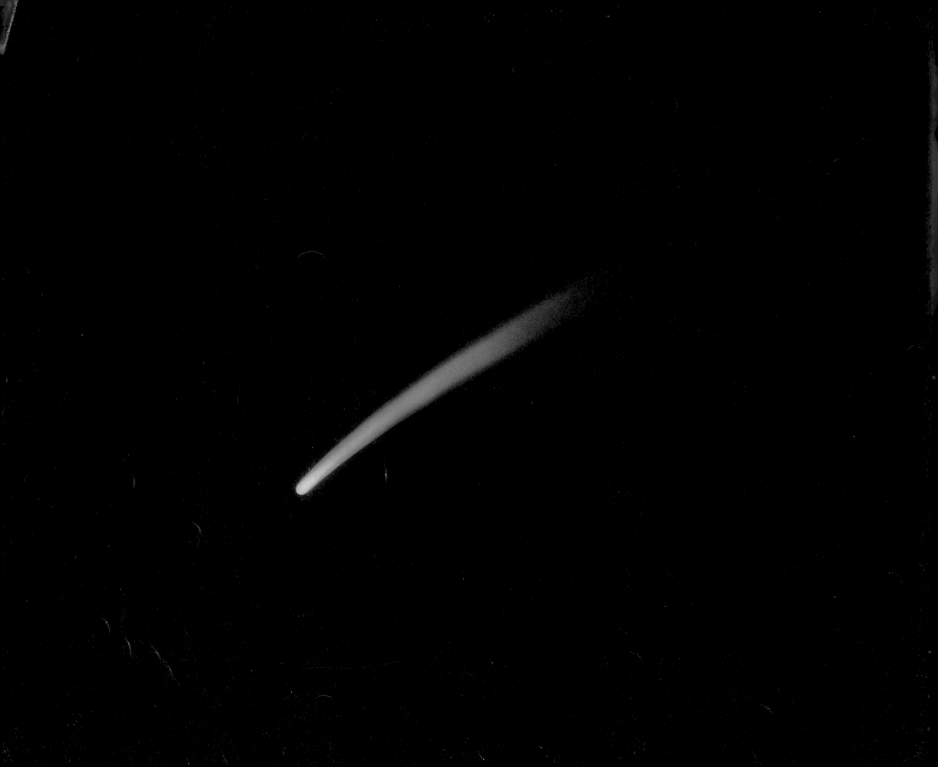

What Is a Comet?

Comets are made of dust, ice, and gas. They **orbit** (OR-bit) around the sun like Earth does. Comets look like stars with cloudy tails of light trailing after them. When a comet passes Earth, it looks like a huge streak of light way up in the sky.

Before people understood what comets were, they were frightened by them. Many people believed that a comet was a sign that something bad was going to happen. But today we know that's not true.

SPACE FACT

Some comets can be seen from Earth over a period of a few days to several months.

◀ A yellow comet gets its name from the color of its tail.

Where Do Comets Come From?

Astronomers (ah-STRON-uh-merz) believe that comets come from a part of the solar system called the **Oort cloud** (ORT CLOWD), which is very far away from the sun. A solar system is a group of planets and other objects in space that circle a star.

The Oort cloud contains material left over from when the solar system was formed. That means comets can tell us a lot about what the solar system was like when it was brand new.

SPACE FACT
The Oort cloud was discovered by a man named Jan Hendrik Oort in 1950.

A nebula, or mass of gases and dust in space, looks like the Oort cloud. ▶

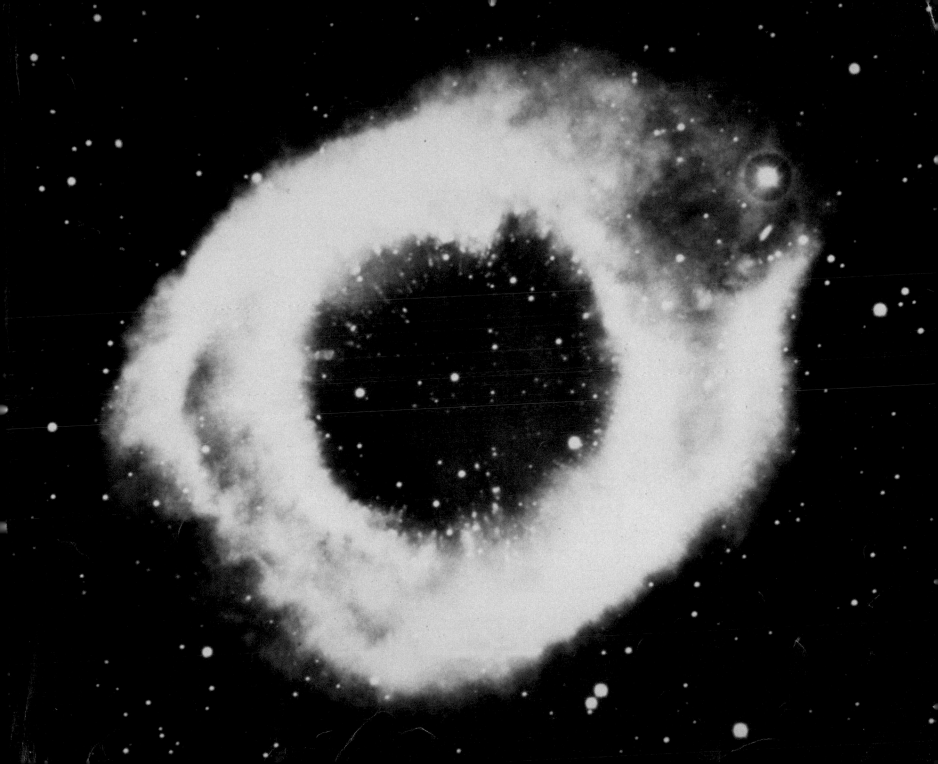

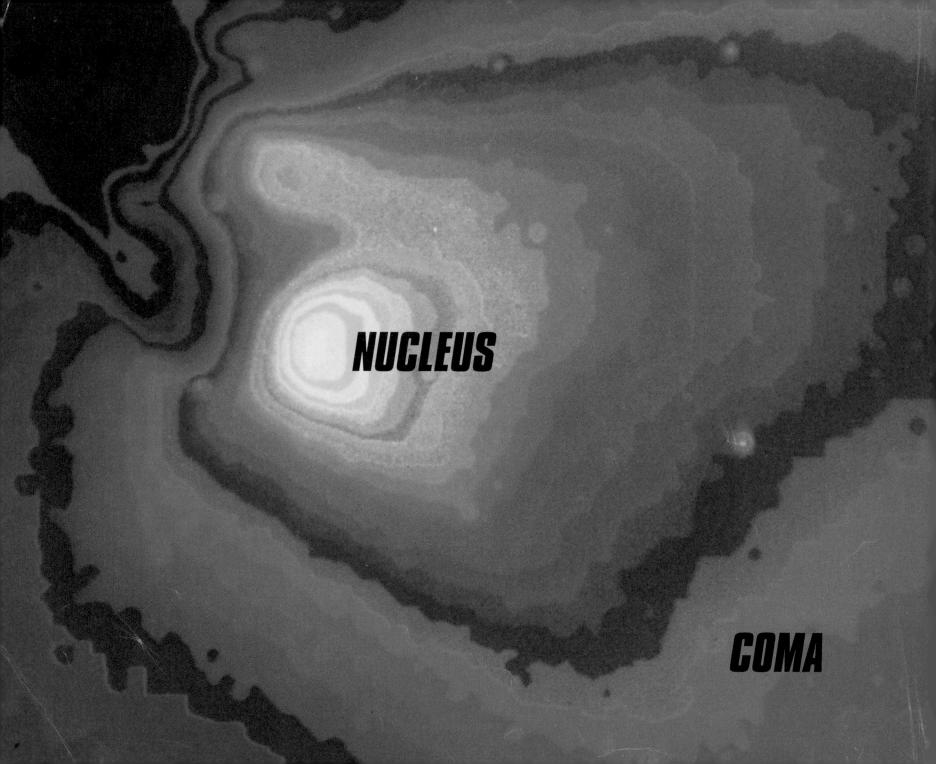

Parts of a Comet

A comet is formed when the **gravity** (GRA-vih-tee) between the sun and the Oort cloud causes dust and ice to come together.

The most solid part of a comet is called the **nucleus** (NOO-klee-us). This small part of a comet is made mostly of frozen gas.

The **coma** (KOH-muh) is a bright ball of gas and dust that surrounds the nucleus. Many tails flow out from the coma. A tail of a comet is made of dust and gas coming off the nucleus. A comet's tail can be as long as 60 million miles!

◀ There are different parts that make up a comet.

The Orbit of a Comet

A comet starts its trip around the sun as a ball of ice, gas, and dust. As it gets closer to the sun, the sun's heat begins to melt the frozen gas in the nucleus. The gas flows off the nucleus in huge streaks that form the tail.

The tail is longest when the comet is near the sun. Tails can be blue, yellow, or white. The tail gets smaller as the comet heads back into space, away from the sun's heat.

SPACE FACT

A comet's tail will always point away from the sun.

The tail of a comet gets shorter as it moves farther away from the sun. ▶

Halley's Comet

Halley's comet is the most famous comet. This comet passes near Earth every 76 years.

Halley's comet is named after an astronomer from England named Edmond Halley. Halley lived from 1656 to 1742. He was the first person to figure out when the comet would return.

The last time Halley's comet passed Earth was in 1986. If you are lucky, maybe you'll get to see it when it comes back in 2061.

In the summer of 1996, a comet called Hyakutake passed over the United States. It was very bright, and could be seen without a telescope. It looked like a starry cloud up in the sky.

◀ There are records of Halley's comet being seen as far back as 1531.

What Is an Asteroid?

Asteroids (AS-teh-roydz) are chunks of rock that orbit the sun just like the planets do. But they are much smaller than planets.

Most asteroids in the solar system are found in the asteroid belt, which is between Mars and Jupiter.

Some scientists believe that the "moons" orbiting other planets are really just asteroids that got caught in the pull of the planet's gravity. The moons around Mars are more like asteroids than they are like Earth's moon.

Most asteroids are located far from Earth, between other planets in our solar system. ▶

How Many Asteroids Are There?

Over 6,000 asteroids have been found and named. Many more exist, but they are too small to see from Earth. Astronomers know of 26 asteroids that are more than 125 miles from one side to the other.

The biggest asteroid known is called 1 Ceres. It is over 550 miles wide. That's the distance from the state of New York to the state of North Carolina!

SPACE FACT

Asteroids orbit the sun just like the planets, but meteors do not.

The moons orbiting some planets, such as Saturn, may actually be asteroids.

What Is a Meteor?

Scientists believe that some meteors are pieces of comets. Others are pieces of asteroids.

Have you ever seen a shooting star? Actually, this is not a star at all but something called a **meteor** (MEE-tee-or). Meteors are rocks and **particles** (PAR-tih-kulz) from space that come to Earth.

Meteors move very fast through space. When a meteor enters the Earth's **atmosphere** (AT-mus-feer), it slows down and heats up. When the meteor gets really hot, it starts to burn and leaves a trail of light that looks like a "shooting star."

A meteor may produce different colors as it burns up. ▶

Meteor Showers and Meteorites

When Earth passes through the tail of a comet, a lot of the tail's dust and rock pieces burn up when they reach our atmosphere. It looks like hundreds of fireworks up in the sky, falling down to Earth. These are called meteor showers.

If a meteor makes it through Earth's atmosphere and lands on the ground, it is called a **meteorite** (MEE-tee-or-yt). Many of these space rocks have been found and studied by scientists.

◀ This meteor is called the Leonid Fireball Meteor.

Using Spacecrafts to Learn About Comets

Only in the last eleven years have we been able to actually use **spacecrafts** (SPAYS-krafts) to explore comets.

These spacecrafts don't carry people in them. Instead, they collect information and take pictures of things in space. Then those pictures are sent back to Earth. The information we get from comets can help us to understand our solar system and how it was formed.

SPACE FACT In July 1994, a comet called Shoemaker-Levy 9 actually crashed into Jupiter! This was the first time we were able to see two space objects crashing into each other.

Glossary

asteroid (AS-teh-royd) Rocky objects in space that orbit the sun and some planets.

astronomer (ah-STRON-uh-mer) A scientist who studies space.

atmosphere (AT-mus-feer) The gases that surround a planet.

coma (KOH-muh) The part of a comet that looks like a bright ball surrounding the nucleus and that is made of gas and dust.

gravity (GRA-vih-tee) The force that comes from an object, like a planet or the sun, that pulls objects toward it.

meteor (MEE-tee-or) A rock or particle from space that enters Earth's atmosphere.

meteorite (MEE-tee-or-yt) When a meteor survives the trip through the atmosphere and lands on Earth.

nucleus (NOO-klee-us) The main part of a comet which is made of ice, gas, and dust.

Oort cloud (ORT CLOWD) A region of the solar system far from the sun where comets are thought to come from.

orbit (OR-bit) How something circles something else.

particles (PAR-tih-kulz) Small pieces of something.

spacecraft (SPAYS-kraft) A spaceship that is sent into space to collect information and take photographs. Some spacecrafts carry people too.

Index